# Polly's Special Day

By

## Yulinda Blake Cook

ISBN 978-1-0980-7178-3 (paperback)
ISBN 978-1-0980-7179-0 (digital)

Christian Faith Publishing
832 Park Avenue
Meadville, PA 16335
www.christianfaithpublishing.com

Library of Congress Control Number: 2022900024

Printed in the United States of America

# Dedication

Hi Mama,

    I named this book after you! I miss you! Let me know what you think!

    To my grandchildren: Jordyn, Charlie, Phoenix, Cager, Cross, Shiloh, Zuri, Boss and Xavier. You are my joy! I love you! YaYa

Hello, my name is Polly!

    My day has just begun. The sun is smiling, and I'm ready for some fun!

Today is a special day, and it belongs to me! My dad told me so, and I totally agree!

Dad said I can eat cake all day from sunup to sundown!

4

I'm Queen for the day! See my sparkly crown?
Normally I'm a princess, but I jumped up a notch!
Uh-oh! It's time for A-C-T-I-O-N, according to my watch!

WOW!
The nerve of it! Who ever heard of it, eating cake all day?
B-R-E-A-K-F-A-S-T is where I'll start.

"Yes!" she said without delay, as
she sang from the kitchen,
    "It's your day! It's your day!"

The pots and pans began to sing; the water began to flow!
There's a symphony in the kitchen. Today is my day, don't cha know!

It's a special day, and that's a fact!
I'll start with pancakes, and that's a stack!

I want syrup, butter, and cinnamon toasted nuts! Give me chocolate chips! Cream that's whipped! Add a glass of cold, cold milk!

Grant me mountains of berries and other fruits—bacon, eggs, and sausage to boot! I…can eat cake all day?! That's what's up!

Mom made my favorite ... C-U-P-C-A-K-E-S!

Big cupcakes, small cupcakes, square cupcakes too! Red cupcakes, orange cupcakes, multicolored and blue!

Cupcakes with sprinkles, cupcakes with crinkles, cupcakes with chips, cupcakes with dips, cupcakes with sparklers, whizzes, and whips!

Cupcakes with icing, some without; so many cupcakes make me want to shout!

So many cupcakes, where do I start? I'm racing like a turtle. I'm playing it smart! Being smart is not eating too much cake, because that will make my tummy ache!

Dad says that everyone deserves a day so grand. They should pick a day and celebrate it, any way they plan.

Welcome ... to Daddy & Daughter's Day

best DAD

BIG MAMA'S KITCHEN & BAKERY

He's taking me on an adventure to different places in town. I can eat cake all day, so I'll take it by the POUND.

P-O-U-N-D C-A-K-E!

Pound cake is a round cake with a hole in the middle.
It's good hot! It's good cold! It's good with peanut brittle.
Some of them have frosting. Some have glaze. Look around you, it's all
a maze!

17

Cakes here, cakes there—cakes, cakes, everywhere! Pink cream…orange dream…key lime. It's lunchtime!

What's next Dad?

Hmmm, I don't have a clue, but I see something
in my view…

L-A-Y-E-R C-A-K-E!
Layers of cake stacked with icing in between, with flavors so royally fit for a queen. This cake has many layers, two or three or more. On my special day, I want twenty-four!

Twenty-four layers, to be exact! Twenty-four colors, can you imagine that?!

Layers with stars, layers with jiggles, layers with faces that make me giggle.

I dream of eating straight to the center, where strawberries and blueberries are!

I'd roll to the left, jump to the right, and chomp upon a star.

Whoa! SKRR ... let me slow down with my little snack. Getting too full would really be Wack!

W-A-C-K-Y C-A-K-E!
This cake is CRAZY and WACKY you see. I looked at it, and it looked back at me! With two BULGING eyes and a BIG crooked smile... OOPS! Oh my! I ate a C-R-O-C-O-D-I-L-E!

23

I ate the eyes; I ate the smile; but crumbs fell on my skirt! Oh, no! Oh no! What shall I do? The crumbs look like dirt!

WACKY CAKES

# DIRT CAKE ASSEMBLY

D-I-R-T C-A-K-E!
Dirt cake is chocolate cake and pudding in a bowl with "worms," "bugs," "slugs," and "sand" refrigerated to stay cold. I know, I know, it sounds so yucky! But take a look and see…

25

The "worms" and "bugs" and "slugs" and "sand" are cookies and gummy candy! I've got to stop, Tick-Tock, Tick-Tock! It's time for us to go home.

EXIT

DIRT CAKE
FINISH LINE

ILLA   WORM   GS SLUGS SAND

This special day with my dad was the BIGGEST SHOW ON EARTH! He said today was all about showing me my worth.

The LOVE I feel for my dad is bigger than the Universe.

We had such fun. We laughed all day. I wish it could go in reverse.

28

P.S. Spending time with family and friends should always be "A Piece Of Cake!"

And that's Polly's Solution!

30

# What are you Celebrating?

PLACE YOUR PICTURES HERE:

DATE:

# About the Author

Yulinda Blake Cook is a wife, mother of four, and Yaya to nine wonderful grandchildren and counting. Professionally and personally, her path has always included children and words. One day, she merged the two, and the results have been beautiful works of art. With every book, Yulinda hopes to help fortify the imagination of children and parents alike.

CPSIA information can be obtained
at www.ICGtesting.com
Printed in the USA
JSHW032123010922
30077JS00002B/10